The Keeper
of Height

The Keeper of Height
Angela McCabe

Barlenmir House

Copyright © 1974 by Barlenmir House
All rights reserved. No part of this book may be reproduced in any form by any means, electronic or mechanical, including photocopying, recording, or information retrieval system, without permission in writing from the publisher.

Barlenmir House, Publishers, New York, N.Y.

ISBN: 0-87929-026-9
Library of Congress Catalog Card Number: 73-92346
First Edition
Printed in the United States of America
Book & Cover Design by Steffan

CONTENTS

Part One

Milkweed / 3
First Song / 4
Water Poem / 5
A Different Blue / 6
Like Grass / 7
Not Only / 8
Letter / 9
Bat Dream / 10
Child / 11
Lure / 12
Pink Whistle / 13
Out There / 14
Our Sad Breasts / 15
Transport / 16
Communion / 17
Stones / 18
Sisters / 19
Aubade / 20
Changing Skins / 21
Engagement / 22
Swing / 23
Dream Child / 24
Salvage / 25
Prairie Moon / 26
Bouquets / 27
Paper Boat / 28
Naming / 29
Homecoming / 30
Doll / 31
What, I Am / 33
There / 34
Gentle Neighbors / 35
What You Said / 36
The Unexpected / 37
Flow / 38

What Is My Own / 39
Fish Dream / 40
Names / 41
The Gift / 42
Mountain / 43
Stick / 44

Part Two

Bloom Street / 47
Blind Adolphus / 48
To Robert In Veracruz / 49
From Lois In London / 50
Back / 51
Movie Magazines / 52
Inside History / 53
World War II / 54
To A Sister / 55
The End / 56

ONE

Milkweed

The milkweed split
floated its feathers over the rising dust

Crying from the north
swans shouldered high gusts as easily as my father
stacking the woodpile

My arms ached
My belly turned to the sky and the swans

Winter drawing on
amid all menace and preparation
he stayed with me like a bird
the flock had lost
a treader of water
smoothed with a long breath from shore to shore

First Song

I might have guessed from his low song
Unwinding
In the barns my father kept

Those first days
When the hay held light
And he lowered his angry weight to me

Water Poem

I grew toward love like a drop of water
on the lip of a faucet

When I fell I seethed a moment
on hot stone

When I gathered I became a cloud
over dry earth

When I fell I vanished forever
in mute dust

A Different Blue

I didn't imagine it

Out of indifferent blue the sun came riding
passed so close I smelt the sweat of his horse
I was turned to a tree or something
I thought he hadn't seen me

Out of a different blue the sun came riding
I was swinging and lifted
in a lariat of light
and we burnt up time and space
living again on the leather of his loins

We set together behind the hills
into the kind of peace
that need not rise tomorrow

We set together
I didn't imagine it

Like Grass

Grass grows longest
In the corner

All winter the tracks had lost themselves
In drifts
Nobody went out

The visitor left footprints round the barn
And out again where the road was swollen

I walk heavier
My heels sinking deeper
Night sour between my breasts

Not Only

It was not summer's weight
or not that only
not only the grosser sleep of earth

Time strained over me
the farm lay flat on its back until
the thunder rolled it over

When harvest came the farm was empty
the voice of storms had forgotten its promises

Then there was only the blood
the loss

Letter

The straw here is wire
as high
along the sleek streets
as our May barn.
This distance
throws you up
behind your team working
the earth with steel
and stone insistence.
The men here
pale as cement
and weak
know nothing of the drag
through stony earth, the silent
weir of birds starting from pepper trees.

Boxed between big business
I'm clutched
by four blank walls in this room.
The life here is polished
steel
honking like geese over the north pond,
movement is oiled.

At night
wrapped in hay
I slip back to be there
when you push in
with the last light from the fields.

Bat Dream

A movement beyond the wall
shakes him from the mountain
a savage sprawling through trees

Where the dark whistles on edge
moss thickens upon wood
the wings beat

And now shuttering the light
the bat
leans for me from the dark

Child

I am a child lost
in a forest of silk screens

the dragons writhe and coil
but their fiery tongues don't touch me

Once I inherited the earth
I was bound to embrace its weight

Now I speak to myself
in a whisper of fingertips

Lure

Your small hand of a child's face
is streaked sad, these strong
arms in tears at your side

Have I rattled coins at your hip?

You cast a lewd bait
to lure my silence to you
with fingers that climb the trellis
beneath the folds of my dress

It is morning when I hear your steps in the rain

Pink Whistle

You will find it in the bookcase
Of a man with many bookcases
On each bookcase there are two
Of every book he owns
Ask him his sign
He will tell you his reading habits
Ask him for the whistle
He will tell you he is going
To kick in your head but
He kisses you gently
And puts his fingers into your mouth

He is ready for more questions
He will answer with your whistle

Out There

There was nothing to call my own

I was a strange moon rolling
a sphere of many waters
in a galaxy of strangers

A swarm of suns
each one sucked at my tides

I was shared out and scattered
my mouth was full of their promises

I woke

A basket of live crabs
in the market of hunger

Our Sad Breasts

Like nothing
they left their pants at the door
bras hung from chairs
I watched them
smoothly
rise bald from manes
for mates
Our sad beasts from their caves
hungered back
Slowly
first one then many
the eyes went out
One by one they disappeared
rocked somewhere from sound
The whole room danced
I put my head back
balancing in the rhythm
that beat time against the floor

Transport

He rides her through applause
The slap of the leather on his chest
Steel behind the toes
His chaps
On her sides
Smooth

He rides her there
Points her nose to the sun
Hands
Pushing him to paradise
Yes
He rides her
Rides her

Communion

A wet fish flapping
A clapper ringing
No bell
Weeds the scythe had missed and hands
Uprooted

Holes in the bank no bird enters
Faces full of fingers
Wasted mouths eating the fish slapping
The bell swinging weeds
Terrible in their meagerness
Useless in their bite

Stones

from all sides
hands
I fling them from me
they are not mine

voices call
that do not even bother to dissemble
they demand
hard
smooth

I turn them over
Each back is crawling

Sisters

You said it is nothing it is easy
no reason to be afraid
it is only the gentlest of whispers
in the body's bower

It is only a clear stream
you said no stone no whirlpool
but softly between silk banks
out of the strident sunlight

So we lay down in lilac
the pollen of my body
fed the bees of your dream

We slept an estuary
where the only boats were fingertips
trailing nets of water

Aubade

In the shadow of her perfume
she makes her face up at dawn
From closets
a scent rises
to ride with dust on light
In lace
I follow
color to color
I silence her with a stroke

Outside
in the barn where my father kept hay
I hear a boy
who knows how the lyric of my life works

Changing Skins

Such quiet in my hips
such silk growing out of me as another skin
over my head

Father
you have ceased flying
I need not hide from you
fearful of your hooks in my hair
that now dresses itself in the mirror
of her thighs closing over me
so my arms grow from my sides
to sway above the bed above the house
above her binding and releasing
above the rhythm of my past

Mother
I found you leaning in the window
I never called to you
I never call to anyone

Engagement

He meets me for dinner with manners.
All right, age spreads like a lung
To encompass every other breathing thing.
Mild as a Millie I once knew, I cut
Through the tenderloin while his knees
Part mine like butter. His tie
Is of an exquisite blue. Silver
Cufflinks charm my sleeve as he pins
Me to the table. Now biscuits
Warm as what waits below the table,
Taped to the waist like a vial.
I'm content to let the wine span
Our difference. He at fifty
Goes off sweet at the tongue
After minced lamb. As mint
Jelly tags his cuff, I fall for him.
Once my father bent to me and let his weight
Become part of mine: strange,
Now this man weighs on me. His knee
Moves past respect—my age,
My lack of age. . . .   I watch him count
The tip into the check. At midnight,
Before the lights, he lifts me
Through an elderly romance. His fire
is a little less than pleasing, fanned
By his own lack of breath. Love
He says is a green apple pinned
To the brow of a cagey girl.

Cagey, I turn from sleep
And call a stranger.

Swing

I am in the swing
only my feet stay aground
I push and the earth moves
I sit still and I move
kicking inside myself
my hands curiously alive
as if itching to draw something out
I only half believe is there
If I believe more fully
I would still stay rooted
to my own fear
tear at myself
at this thing
they will call
mine
this darkness soaking beneath my waist
that will thin my lips
coil me inside out
leave me reeking
forever of a death
not my own choice

As I push at the swing
this is my own death I am rocking

Dream Child

I've dreamt you dropping forever
clotted
not maroon liquid
sliding away
I've seen you propped hanging
between my legs
then pulled from me in a scream
your face named
and part of another part
of my life
We've talked
the two of us standing on a shout
that is eaten by the
void
filling me like an echo
But you are always flowing
less than something
climbing for earth out of the red
wall you won't embrace
I've been dreaming you forever
your dark hair
your small voice calling me by name

Salvage

I remember you in the kitchen
holding your heaving coat
grinning a pair of sodden boots
"What goddam weather"

And in the barn where you were master
among the salvage of toil
when I was a young owl in the rafters

Mother fretted about you
I could see it even then
and when you leant over my bed
your goodnight left me wakeful

I have felt you time and again
touch my skin with history
here on my bed away from home
where I sit and read the letter

It took an electric typewriter
to tell me in black and white
that you had died forever

I launch a ship of dreams

Prairie Moon

I have found this stick and am beating around with it
There are no bushes and the air is a poor provider

I have found a bush and am flailing it
but the bush has a shadow that is fighting back

In the dark I am tangling the looseness of air
I bring down a flap of skin with my long stick

I step inside and am a swan's breast
shadow of the moon slipping off to the west

Bouquets

Hayropes and daisychains—
do you remember how I left them by the pond
and you, you sent me back
to fetch them?

I fetched them

They had blown onto the water
strung out like snakes or eels
waterlogged
I threw stones to sink them

I sat down to weave pebbles and burrs
into some frayed twine I found in the old hut

I left the bouquet for you on the table
you who had no use for bouquets
except those you
gave

Paper Boat

How are the years?

Can one call them sunk or lost
if they are all one has

Five years are five fingers
whose print is everywhere
on my face
smeared on the inside of my belly
stuck somewhere between two rocks

Somebody's print is on me
on this paper boat
and I ask
when will the wind turn
drive me back on myself
take my hand
and smash it down on the boat
nearer to no shore
sleeper in no sails

Naming

I search among the split ends

I lay the forehead bare

Have I allowed myself the luxury of no identity?

Where would I have gone if not here?

I face the world made up of many splinters

Where are the parts of those who knew me?
Have I eaten them?
Those who took me by the name and shook it out
folded it like a napkin each his own way

Where do I look?

My hair is dark and grows too much
Scissors lie over lipstick on my dresser
Lipstick must go
scalp be laid bare

Where was I born?

Who told me what I was?
                        I will shear and pare to bone
                        My name will not be mine

Homecoming

I lost myself in steel and stone
rectangular stone stare
that looked right through me

The lights went streaming uptown
too fast to notice the sidewalk
where I cast no shadow

I came to myself in a small room
I had already forgotten
a white cloud on a blue bed

I stretched myself out head to toe
belly to belly
so I came home

I entered in at the mouth

The eyes also were open

Doll

I seem to have carried you around
forever
stuck in the corner of cases
next to the one or two books I use
as ballast
You with your barn-red hair
and face smooth as a fence-post
thousands of cattle have rubbed themselves against

You sit beside the window
legs stuck out as if broken
by some monstrous fall
dress patched calico
flesh unreal as regrets
pink as a prairie dawn
when night still lashes the back of the horizon
and birds still rise in long V's
to plough their way to the sun
or the moon
or wherever the sky is easiest

What do you see?
Button eyes see only buttons
though our faces have seen each other so long
we can call each other our own
but what can we call our own
except our death?

You have watched and said nothing
What you haven't seen you can guess at
from what you know

I gave you that cracked head
those few fingers
those ridiculous clothes

I wait for you to come apart
drop into your silly pieces
of cloth and plastic
It is time for you to be discarded anyway

The Lord giveth and the Lord taketh away

What, I Am

Yes
her name is part of the unnameable
part of the push
or circling in the very way things have
of becoming what they might never have become
All right
she has bedded down with the deadliest
come up without a thorn
clean as myth
She splays herself in the old stocks
New England fuckery
saints behind the maple wood
an English tongue dipped in snow

I am my own flesh moving on bone
my own hair curling
beyond superstition
In my body I am what I have never been
a simple cycle
of what in the end we become
The feel of the cloth I wear
measures how I feel about myself
Satin is the weight
upon my breasts
Everywhere I am
everything I might have been or will become
Filling
or filling again
that old chamber with the hot air

There

They play with their hands here
for hours
afloat on fingers of boredom
Their smiles come in odd shapes
appear at strange intervals
The attendants are bleached
everything is pleasant
but stripped of anything pleasing
The letters from your own brittle world
click like plastic
We eat on plates that are almost rubber
The others
will try anything
slice their features
with any sharp edge in reach
Everything here is soft but your flowers were
armed with a scent
that set the patients on edge
Remember how you told me
when you held me then before you left
that you were not the thief of my words?
Our wounds will open their lips to each other
when the doors open
and I come through the padding
holding your name, a caramel in my mouth

Gentle Neighbors

These strangers are more welcoming than relatives
their smiles are whiter
the buttons undo more easily

their hands move more easily onto my skin
under the atrocious sweater
that kept me separate

In corridors of clean linen
I glide out on my charitable errands
you are worlds unto yourselves my gentle neighbors
I waken you with daylight

I am the soft lawn where your eye can rest
I am the open door of your tomorrows
I am the shuffle of cards

I loosen the collar of night
I am the form you see my gentle neighbors
when you stare in the untroubled pool
in the garden you cannot remember

Believe in me

What You Said

You said
      don't give the whole thing
it is good to be naked strangers

You said
      when you get to my age
you'll find your nakedness
smooth with the leather of failure

You said
      take what you can from me
give only what comes easily
don't let me paint a bruise on you
with the brush of my indifference
I have forgotten the fairy-tales
that whispered in my pillow

I said
      it doesn't matter
      it doesn't matter
I said again and again
      it doesn't matter

The Unexpected

I thought it would turn with slow regret
and shake its head at me
that morning when I came home
to the room you had left your prints on

The chair where you had put your clothes
held out its arms to no purpose
and the bed untouched since then
had fallen from our laps to where it was

But the room was full and unexpected
you'd let yourself in with the key I'd meant to give you

This being alone is a lie
      If there's a place where you are not with me
I have never been there

Flow

Where does the music go

In the mine I hear veins correspond with veins
and feel trees carry sounds
up the straight trunk
to spread throughout air's bright shell

I am in these trees
I am diffused in air
You have turned me in the dark
as the seasons turn
We have played among my roots
where I had lived too long
fettered
in a fairytale

Now the sap rises
and I flow into wooden cups

Any wound made
will become bark

What Is My Own

Neither heavy nor light
moved
here to a door and there a window

I suppose I set the table
acts accustomed to fingers
I smooth the sheets
into a skin as much like mine

But cotton is hostile
I roll in my own cocoon
my own warmth wearies me
I turn to liquid

But even darkness cups me
I am held in my own shape
restless as I may be

Until I look in the mirror
me and today are one thing
and yet

it takes a different hand it seems
to trace my outlines for me.

Fish Dream

The railing is a keeper of height

Knee deep
she wades farther
as the ocean spreads
its dream of silence

the leap through water
into sleep

She dreams herself into the green
water
breathing with bass
her movements touching
the pale flesh of
fish in an undertow
that drifts for darkness

Names

What shall I call you
belly-hopper
jumping-jack
whippoorwill in the grass
calling me in and out

Hop O' My Thumb you say
Well I'll try it
but where I land
is my concern

I ask nothing of where you come from
green man
Where you go interests me only so long
as why I go with you

I prefer to call you by made-up names

The Gift

That morning arrived without you
or rather
you put on your shoes before he did

I won't see you again it seems
stranger who learnt so soon to speak my body
with a perfect accent

Now in the accustomed autumn of your absence
something budges
a leaf that should be asleep turns in my belly

I turn stones over with my foot
I look at the damp hollows they have sheltered
I count the days

Mountain

Take the mountain
and when you've got a focus on it
focus again

So he said
I looked
So small it was
you could have swung a cat around it
so large
years were in each stone and each rock
was a head

I had never seen it totally till then
though it had been rising like a seabeast
at every twist of my hand

He said
mountains are born
the tallest are still babies
I said
the young are jagged
there are chasms no one knows of
the rumble in the night is often
part of the mountain collapsing into itself

When the young erode
there is nothing to impede their fall
and they have farthest to drop

Stick

With this stick
I stir pools
and winter puts its mouth
to the window

I write with winter
water
cleansing the point
fire hardened

The window has opened
Swallows come to perch
where they never did
The stick sprouts

Now I can
wave its leaves
anywhere
Walls open
and the room is all air

TWO

Bloom Street

I will remember you on Bloom Street as you stood
in front of the Pontiac showcase, in the brown suit
you wore for weddings and all rites of passage. Did they
bury you in brown? Did they pack your strong white legs
together and wind them in burlap brown? Did they press
your hard knees and iron down the blisters on your
crooked toes and gentle your neck with dull copper
flocking? Brown. This is the odor of transience.
I cannot remember the color of gold on fire; I will not
remember the sound of your voice in my hand.

Blind Adolphus

I remember Longwood. I remember driving there
to see Clara and mother's blind cousin, Adolphus, in
the spring, at Longwood, in the Dynaflow. I recall
how we stayed at a Tudor Style Inn, near Grand
Rapids, and the way the walls there were stained. They
looked like Champ Levee, though somewhat irregular,
patterns of the fleur de lys, in the mellow early
evening light before I could settle down to sleep,
and the next day, Longwood. I recall the avenue of
Longwood, and how it seemed never to end, and the
muffler dragged on the ground, and when we got to
Longwood it was all like a negative, everybody
dressed in wheat clothes with white faces and Clara,
bleached out, came onto the terrace and seemed
to have about her a flock of white doves, though,
when she came closer, I could see they were just
tissues, for she had a cold or so it seemed to me, and
Daddy said why, Emmaline she looks all got up for
a *Wedding* and Momma, did she have a cold, too?
she laughed and didn't sound exactly happy. We
went inside. It smelled of cellar, old damp books
crying in a cellar. All the furniture was put in rows
alongside the wall. Echo of Auntie Clara's voice:
Adolphus is in there, it's cooler in the pantry. In the
pantry he was lying on the old zinc table. Uncle
Adolphus. And Momma holding me back. And
Clara puts her finger to her lips. I remember Uncle
Adolphus, his hair flowing over the end of the table,
and his eyes wide open and they stare at his feet,
not seeing anybody, and of course they wouldn't
because he's blind. And I recall how I thought oh at
last, at last now I know what a blind man is, and
thinking how fine a thing to be blind, you can just
lie on the pantry table and stare at your feet if you
want and no one can talk or disturb you. Mother
said, "Well, he had thirty-four *good* years. . .".

To Robert In Veracruz

You don't begin to know the reasons why I love
you. Your so-called strength, oh you *are* strong,
your sheer appropriateness, propriety is what you've
named it, and your acumen behind the wheel
of your little Triumph, these acquisitions of which
you despair that are the weapons that my love lies
down before. I love you when you fail. Your
appropriateness took you away to some
brime-softened port where I can only imagine you
will melt into what you despise, something soft,
perhaps? Please then keep your hardware, let me
be your soft belly, your shy and deprecating
murmur, your unexpected laugh, your grief. . . .

From Lois In London

Angela Honey (she wrote) I would it were not so
but baby I'm broke and there's nothing worse than that
unless it's being bankrupt I don't know about the latter
but let me tell you what happened. There's nothing
worse than being broke in London on a lukewarm day,
dig? So I walked out into the smogshine and felt like I
was the spirit of food rationing itself, pale after a war,
no color in the margerine, and I kept forgetting and
walking off the kurb? And these things, these micro
minis that they've got around here, whip past and toot
the juice through you, something I'm in no shape
to handle, and so I went into St. James park which is
the park where Billy Graham caught a couple going
at it and where on any lukewarm day the grass heaves
with sex, which I don't harbour any prejudices against,
only wishing I could have a hand in the old moil, when
Mr. Jack-the-Ripper himself comes along. Sits down.
Raincoat and no jockeys syndrome the whole bit. So
we're sitting there, side by side, and nothing happens.
I mean nothing. A real Antonioni. I guess he knows
I'm broke. Finally, out of utter boredom, I turned
and said, "Well aren't you going to say something,
do anything, touch and feel?" Angela, dig this:
He said, luv, I'm off duty, so I thought I'd try to
give you a bit of cheer, you look so glum. Thanks,
that's nice, I said. And then he reached into the
trench coat, and I thought okay honey here goes,
and you know what? He pulled out a *Sock*!! he said,
it was a real old flesh colored knitted golf sock, I'll
have to present you with this because it's all I've got,
but it'll get you a meal somewhere. I was all set to
say feh! take that vile thing away, when he told me
in the gentlest voice, "This was the sock Wellington
had on when he won the battle at Waterloo." I just
wanted to tell you that in case the world was too
much with you, regards, Lois.

Back

Of course when someone leaves you forever you
see his back. I could have hit it with a cannonball but,
still, there it would have remained: his bristly jacket
pinched around the shoulders, the bladed tweed grimace
of a retreat, a back with a face, I imagined, that forced
off it "I cannot."

    Had I left him, and lost the game, would he have
longed after my mourning back? No, he would have
preferred to think how nonchalant I am, and turned
away, maybe even smiling. Later, taking off his jacket,
and rubbing his shoulder, he would tell a friend, "How
much easier it is for women. Water off a goddamned
duck's back."

Movie Magazines

In my dream movie I'm a little tiger pussy bathing princess of the adolescent bra and lace doily panties, prancing round a plastic swim tank in our old backyard with Johnnie Gripsholm and Martin Spewer, a regular Lorelei with her slender blackhaired Italianate boy (Johnnie Gripsholm adopted by the town Superintendant out of Italian orphanage at age of about three, so has wildly independent though utterly frivolous tendency to rebellion) and her blond puppy lover, doing the old boop a loo, catch-as-catch-can, just like a little Tuesday Weld (Tuesday and I are about the same age come to think of it, only my scars *show*) before she learned to read. Later it turns out the dream movie star sleeps between dirty lines and drives herself in her own Camaro across the Mohave, to Las Vegas, or is that only where they get married. I like to think I learned to read too late.

Inside History

History she (Zelda) said stops here. The efforts of history don't belong here, that is true, but there are tangibles.

Last night after they turned the lights out (we are forty women, laid side by side on our backs on white enamelled cot beds like tomb effigies who breathe only in darkness together) I saw history on black velvet: the fires of our flat Autumns tore down the farm house in my eyes, a bicycle child swerved in terrific wind, blinded I suppose by the heat, into the belly of our kitchen stove, instinctively looking for some kind of ashen warmth away from the heat. She heard bellows from her father's room: Don't go there (where? She was standing quite fine in a white nightdress on a silent burnt landscape, bicycle dead like a dog at her feet but unburnt.) Her mother's hand combed her tangled hair. She was all caring.

"You must look your very very best," she said. "And now we will go and see what happened to your father."

World War II

>   (Page from diary after seeing *The Longest Day* with L.L. and Chico).

Why do they think only they have a premium on Tanks and Guns? I asked Chico and she said well they don't do they and I said I don't think I get you or some such thing and she said well they don't, you know? Because I have a Mauser automatic and a collection of grenades that would fill a cellar somewhere and I couldn't believe it and then L.L. said yeah man I know what you mean I've been collecting that stuff too and I got a lot more where that comes from *What* are you two girls talking about? I said I mean I was pretty surprised I mean dream movies and dream movies and L.L. said when did you come out of the woodwork kiddo? I have about seven MI rifles I got from the armory when they tore it down and My Dad when we went to Normandy he got the German Corporal we went with he and My Dad got to be best buddies after the war and they have a reunion at all the battle sites, one each year, they reminisce, you know? It's vile she said but he gave me a Lüger to keep as a memory of him. And if I wanted he'd go to the trouble to get me a tank I know it. Because it's better to have the fifth column on your side, I guess.

To A Sister

If I were not such a little sister myself I could comfort you more. I haven't got anything more than you do and now I know I have less than I did when I came here. When I came here I felt whole, anyway. I don't feel whole anymore. The way people look at me when I walk: How I wish it could be that I felt substance, something I could swing around. . . . C. left me after giving me more, and took all the pulse away with him, what beat inside me, what made parts of me collide softly when I came across a room to meet him, fullness, hope turning slowly and waking up. I'd get warm right away. Certain parts feel empty in ways that won't refill, I know, because inside they are hard, as a lung becomes hard before you cease to breathe.

    Keep those parts. Don't give them to someone else. Instead, give him yourself; that way you'll get it all back when he takes himself away. I used to think those were parts that he gave to me, but now, too late, I see that they were mine all along.

The End

Is this how it will all end then? In slow coming apart, and the spreading stealthy stain of graduated corruption? With "do this just once, this one thing, it's all perfectly on the level," and "Let's just this once try it, what harm is there in that?" And then you do, and afterwards you say, well that was that, I mean why not? It didn't mean anything. What difference does it make. Not even a lie. I wouldn't call it lying. More like stealing. There are all different kinds of stealing. Jean Genet was a thief. To steal is to show your contempt for a basically corrupt society. It's the last bastion of free will. To be a criminal, and at large, that's the best thing to be, actually, no an arid poetess alone, and scarred by her indecisions. Then let's let go. Let's do anything and extract everything we can out of life. We will become creatures of abandon. And abandon ourselves forever to a discoloring sea. Later it's just the same anyhow.

ABOUT THE AUTHOR

Angela McCabe was born on a small farm in Nebraska in 1951. She has been employed as an artist's model in New York City and a waitress in a New Mexico café. This marks the first publication of her work. Her address is usually care of four particular male writers who have encouraged her poetry, and who prefer to remain anonymous at this time.